EXTRAORDINARY GIRL, PHENOMENAL WORLD

50 Motivational Quotes for Living Life Like a Queen

Aisha Freeman

10-10-10 Publishing

Extraordinary Girl, Phenomenal World:
50 Motivational Quotes for Living Life Like a Queen

Published by:
10-10-10 Publishing
455 Apple Creek Boulevard
Suite 200
Markham, Ontario
L3R 9X7

First 10-10-10 Publishing paperback edition 2019
Second 10-10-10 Publishing paperback edition 2019

Table of Contents

Foreword

Are you living your best life? Or are you allowing circumstances, people or habits to stand in the way of who you really are? If so, how do you plan to change that?

Would you like to learn more about a person who has experienced both good and bad circumstances, but has used them for her benefit? No matter who you are or what your current situation is, regardless of your age, culture, or financial situation, *Extraordinary Girl, Phenomenal World* is full of insights and will guide you to fulfill your purpose of living like a Queen.

Author Aisha Freeman shares with you all her personal experiences to help you to overcome distress and move to the place you wish to live. She wholeheartedly believes that you deserve to live your best life, regardless of your past.

Raymond Aaron
New York Times Bestselling Author

About the Author

Aisha Freeman is a health educator and a prominent community leader, best known for hosting community enrichment and empowerment camps in Houston, TX, for adolescent and teenage girls between the ages of 12 and18.

Born in Longview, Texas, Aisha discovered her calling very early in the field of health and wellness. She earned her Bachelors of Science degree, majoring in biology. She then went on to receive her Masters of Science in biology, with a concentration in community health and public health.

While in Louisiana, she worked with many non-profit and for-profit organizations, which later improved her skillset as a community leader. While working in the community, Aisha met many young girls that seemed to not only be broken mentally but also spiritually and physically. This prompted her to begin mentoring girls daily with words of encouragement and group empowerment sessions that consisted of self-help and team building exercises focused on self-esteem and self-worth. As the empowerment sessions grew, so did Aisha's desire to help and motivate young women of today. Now, utilizing both skillsets, of health and community outreach, she continues to motivate and inspire young girls and young women to reach their goals amid any trial or circumstance.

Aisha's number one goal is to ensure that young girls and women live their lives as the Queens that they're designed to be.

About the Book

Changing your thoughts will eventually change your mind. Whether your dream is to become the first generation graduate of your family, to be a world traveler, or to simply be an accountant, *Extraordinary Girl, Phenomenal World* is the motivational blueprint for you.

Aisha Freeman is a young inspiration, who knows how hard it can be to remain positive when tough situations arise. Since she began her love for health and wellness, along with community engagement, at the age of 16, Aisha has faced her share of pressures and obstacles, handling each of them with courage and charm.

In her first ever book, *Extraordinary Girl, Phenomenal World: 50 Motivational Quotes for Living Life like a Queen*, Aisha encourages women to remain positive throughout every situation. This book features Aisha's answers to real life situations about relationships, goals, and faith. Perfect for readers 14 and up, *Extraordinary Girl, Phenomenal World* will empower girls and women to remain positive while pursuing their goals and achieving their dreams.

Chapter 1

You Are a Queen

*"Think like a Queen. A Queen is not afraid to fail. Failure is
another stepping stone to greatness."*
– Oprah Winfrey

Introduction

When I was eleven years old, I told myself that I wanted to be a
great motivational speaker. At the time, I didn't know who I
would be speaking to or what I would be speaking about, but I
knew that I wanted to be great. As time progressed, I became
engrossed in every class project. This included group
presentation, class experiments and, eventually, Prezi
presentations. Before every big project or presentation, I would
always become severely nervous and anxious, but I was prepared.
Weird, right? How can you be nervous and prepared all at the
same time? However, as soon as I clicked on the first slide, or
opened my mouth to utter my first point, all of those emotions
were gone. And every time I present, I think of that same eleven-
year-old girl that wanted to be a great speaker. Now, that girl
knows who and what she will be talking about, and who she will
be talking about it with. That's you!

Hey, Queen! I'm so happy that you decided to get this book. I wrote it specifically for you! In my twenty-seven years of life, I have faced hardships, trials, and some outright unique situations. However, I have also had many amazing, uplifting, and astonishing miracles that even I couldn't have imagined happening. So when I say that this book is for you, it is for you. I want to encourage you! I realize that we are all at different stages of our lives, but if I could tell my eleven-year-old self things that I now know at twenty-seven, things would be a little different.

Furthermore, this book was designed to help my fellow Queens understand how to somewhat navigate through life, based on some of my experiences, which may be known to you or may be a foreign experience. This book holds quotes that have helped me, and quotes that I use on a daily basis to remain inspired.

I challenge you as you read, to reflect on each quote and see how it can be beneficial in your life, or how it can be used to help someone else in their life. As Queens, it is our duty to not only get ourselves together but to also uplift our fellow Queens.

I am rooting for you.

As we embark on this journey together, the one important thing that you must remember is that all time is good time; meaning that the process may be slow, but it's worth it (meaning that your dreams, career, spouse, or fitness goals may be slow, but it is worth it). You must simply stay the course.

Again, I'm rooting for you, Queen—let's go!

Chapter 2

Everyday Life Skills

"You may encounter many defeats, but you must not be defeated. In fact, it may be necessary to encounter the defeats, so you can know who you are, what you can rise from, how you can still come out of it."
– Maya Angelou

Introduction

Has anyone ever made you feel as if you had to be perfect? As if your best wasn't good enough? Well if you haven't before, I hope you never have to experience this. In my case, however, this has happened to me far too often.

Growing up, I was labeled—not necessarily in a bad way, but I was labeled. I was labeled as the girl with the parents that work in the hospital, the girl that has to be a doctor because her dad is a doctor, and the girl that is super smart just because of these labels. Granted, most of those labels aren't bad. Of course, we want to be great like our parents, or even to achieve things that our parents couldn't imagine. However, in my eyes, a label is just a label. No matter good or bad, no one wants to be categorized, placed in a box, or justified by someone else's standards of who or what they should be. So, to challenge everyone, I decided to break those labels. I dared to do the opposite of everything that anyone thought I should do.

Now, don't get me wrong; if you have a dream that falls under a label that someone has given you, that's okay. However, don't let that label someone has placed on you limit your dream.

Sometimes in life, people will put expectations on you that they expect you to have for yourself, and letting them down is usually not the easiest thing to do. As you venture through this first set of quotes, think of your personal challenges and ways that you can overcome them. It can be anything from changing your goals to breaking a habit, or to trying something new.

Whatever it is that you're dealing with, just know that it takes one day at a time to get over it and to overcome it. Don't be labeled, Queen.

Day 1 "You must adapt and overcome."

Do you remember the first time you started something? Think back to your first job or your first day of high school or college. Now think about the feelings you had: uneasy, excited, and overjoyed. Everyone's first day of something is always different. For some people, their first day on the job could be really exciting, or it could be somewhat of a headache, with the new paperwork and first-day agendas.

However, it doesn't matter if it is your first day or your last day of something; you must always adapt and overcome. As situations arise, you must learn to flow with the ocean and ride the wave—you can't dwell on one seat when there is a whole row of seats to be filled, and you must continue in the midst of it all. Queen, this simply means that you must adjust your crown and keep your stride. Yes, hardships happen, and the weather changes, but you must always overcome.

Day 2 "Self-worth, self-love, and self-perseverance. You need all three."

When I was in the third grade, someone called me ugly. No big deal, right? Typically, during our adolescent and teenage years, we are growing and developing from the inside out; so, typically, the term, *ugly*, could never be a true definition for anyone. However, as a young African American child at a private elementary school in Texas, that word can mean a lot.

As you grow, and as you begin to have a true love for yourself, you will understand the meaning of value, and you will further place emphasis on your value as well. Self-worth is how you feel about yourself. Self-love is the love that you inflict on yourself, and self-perseverance is the drive or determination that you have for yourself. You have to understand that if you have love for yourself, then you will never let anyone love you less, and if you know your worth, you will never forget that you're always worthy, no matter what.

Day 3 "Focus on today."

What are you thinking about right now? Your upcoming exam? When your light bill is due, or what you'll have for dinner for the week? Stop, and focus on *right now*. Our minds tend to think ten days ahead of today, and our eyes tend to follow. You've got to focus on the present. Remember that the time you have right now, you can never get back; so use it wisely, and get done what you can today.

Day 4 "Be better than yesterday and greater than the day before."

Every year, around January, you hear, see, and discuss your New Year's resolutions, and everyone has the hashtag, *new year, new me*. They are plastered somewhere in your agenda or in every Facebook status of the New Year. Now, don't get me wrong; setting goals is great, but when we lose sight of those goals, we have to start again.

Each day, you get a chance to refocus and do it better than the day before. This could be anything: work progress, improving in a sport, or even increasing your physical fitness and eating habits. Queen, the goal is to get better each day and to continue to thrive.

Day 5 "Know when to let go."

Letting go is one of the hardest things you will do, but it is also one of the most freeing things that you will do.

My transition from high school to college was rough. I was nervous, excited, and anxious about who I would meet, and if I would make any friends. The tough part about it was that I was stuck in my head; meaning that I was too concerned about the how and the why, and not simply just doing it. This is why it is important to let go. You will find yourself constantly worrying over something you cannot change or haven't even started yet. I challenge you to simply start by first letting it go.

Whatever it is, Queen, you just have to let it go and walk into the new thing.

Day 6 "Choose your battles wisely; remember, war is coming soon."

Everyone has heard the saying that we must choose our battles wisely, right? This typically means that we should learn to walk away from certain situations and not make it an issue by engaging all the time.

This is a skill that we need every day because we are constantly in a battle zone, and there will be issues that arise, but no one ever talks about the war. The battles prepare you for what is ahead. So, yes, Queen, choose your battles wisely so that you are prepared for the war.

During your freshman year of college and high school, you will take a series of entry level courses. Then, as you progress, the entry level becomes second level, then third, and finally, advanced. Those entry courses are preparing you for the war that you will face in your final exams, comprehensive exams, and maybe even your dissertation.

Day 7 "Consistency is the key to everything."

When you first hear a major story about success, what are the first words that most people say? They usually begin with, "I started here," with a goal "to end there." And then, when asked what they did to achieve and obtain these final results, they always say, "I was consistent."

Queen, as your journey down this path called life, it will be easy to feel that you can't do it, or that maybe it wasn't meant for you, but if you have a goal or dream in mind, you must see it through and always do your part—which is to be consistent.

Day 8 "Direction, not intention, will determine your destination."

How many times have you logged into your cell phone GPS, only to find that you already knew the way to get there? Instead of following your own instincts, you decided to use this technology so that you would ensure a successful arrival. Just like the GPS we use to navigate to get somewhere successfully, we must also rely on proper direction in our daily lives to reach our goals and dreams, and allow our vision to come to life. If we simply rely on the intention of getting somewhere, it will never happen. Get your head into the right resources, right people, and right friends, and your direction will align.

Day 9 "Pruning season is helpful for every day cleansing."

In 2019, it seems like everyone is trying to detox, declutter, and clean out everything in their bodies, their closets, and even their relationships. A lot of times, in this cleansing process, there are steps that you must take daily in order to achieve the level of cleansing that is directed. Once that is done, you then, hopefully, can see the results that you were lacking from when you first began the cleanse. So, how are cleansing and pruning similar? To prune is usually defined as cutting the dead, overgrown branches from a tree or plant. Just like how we want to cleanse our bodies of fat, we also have to cleanse our minds of thoughts, old habits, friends, and sometimes family, in order to achieve what we want to achieve. Daily pruning helps you get to where you want to be, because you are constantly cutting off that dead weight that has been hanging on for far too long. Let it go, Queen.

Day 10 "Life is tough, but so are you."

When you sit back and reflect on your life, what are some things you think about? Your losses, your gains, or maybe people that contributed to the two? Or do you think of all your successes and how close you are to finally meeting your goal?

Whatever you reflect on that has happened in the past stages of your life, remember that it is only the past. You have so much ahead of you. If we continue to only look at what once was, we will forget who we could become. This is why we know life is tough, but based on where you are now—still standing, still living and thriving—so are you. You didn't come this far to simply give up.

Day 11" Change begins with you!"

When I moved to Houston, in 2017, I was terrified—not because it was a big city and that traffic is literally always bumper to bumper from the hours of 6 A.M. to 6 P.M.—I was terrified because it required change. I had to change my address, change my route to work, and simply just change my mindset of how I'd always done things. Transitioning from any major point in your life can be emotionally draining, both positively and negatively, but it is usually a catalyst for what we need in order to grow, develop, and take that step closer to who we want to become. So take that leap of change and start today, so you will get to where you need to be tomorrow.

Day 12 "Turmoil produces the best versions of yourself."

When I think of the word, *turmoil*, I immediately think of a thick, black, oily goop that you usually see after buildup occurs in cars, when something hasn't been cleaned properly or something has been denied for a period of time. With this concept in mind, I reflect back on one of the hardest moments of my life, when I was faced with my first ultimatum. I had the choice of doing A or B. Depending on what I chose would determine an outcome that could affect me permanently. Even with the pressure of making the right decision, I still knew that I would face some sort of turmoil; and with that turmoil, I would have to do some cleaning.

As you go through different phases of your life, you will realize that sometimes your decisions will consist of A or B, and you won't be able to choose both. But the defining part is not in the answer you choose, but it is how you treat your *turmoil*. You can let it hinder you, OR you can allow it to create and mold you. Queen, don't give in to the turmoil; instead, clean it up and allow it to work for your good, so that you come out a better version of yourself.

Chapter 3

The Steps to Growth

"You're not obligated to win. You're obligated to keep trying to do the best you can every day."
– Marian Wright Edelman

Introduction

Within my twenty-seven—almost twenty-eight—years of life, I've learned that you never stop growing. As with growth, comes change, and with change, comes new beginnings and endings. The hardest thing for me to digest as I've grown, and continue to grow, is that oftentimes family, friends, and sometimes your community, do not grow with you. Over the years, I've had a bad habit of trying to hold on to things of the past, people of the past, and certain things of the past. By holding on to these things, I have sometimes stunted my own growth, confused myself, and even questioned why I needed to grow or bring them along in the first place.

Queen, as you begin new ventures in life, and take off on your journey, you have to focus in on three important things. The first thing is your immediate circle. Who are your friends? What are your friends trying to achieve? How are your friends affecting you? This is major for all Queens, whether you're in college, middle school, or adult life. These questions are pretty easy; your circle around you is usually trying to graduate from college, get a job, and buy that car they've talked about for years. But what about after college friends, or those friends you get when you start high school, or the friends you have that never go to college. How are they affecting you? Remember, the circle that we keep around us, has the biggest impact on us.

The next thing to remember is to keep your dreams and goals in clear view. While your immediate circle is pivotal to your growth, so is the setting and establishment of your goals. From elementary school to middle school, to college and beyond, your goals may change, alter slightly, or even completely take a left turn, but you must still keep them in your sight. Having these at the forefront of your plan will help you gain things that wouldn't seem possible if you didn't have them. Your goals and dreams don't have to be picture perfect to write them down—but you must write them down and keep them in the forefront. The last thing to focus on is loving yourself as you grow. It's one thing for others to not accept you, but when you don't accept yourself, that's when things will get tough, and it will be hard to go through.

Queen, as you progress through your stages of growth, you must accept that it is first a process that is ongoing, but you can get through it as long as you remain true to who you are, and understand the company that you keep around you.

Again, it is called growth for a reason—each stage will not be like the next. Keep your head up; you will win.

Day 13 "Progress leads to progression."

I used to get so frustrated when I didn't achieve my goals. I used to think that I was a failure, and that the goals I set were either too high or weren't meant for me to reach them. However, in the midst of my failure, I failed to understand the progress that I had made through the journey of trying to obtain the goal. Realize this, Queen: Any time you set out on your goal or vision, there will be a one-step, two-step, or even twenty-step process to get to what it is you are trying to obtain. As you continue to go up that ladder, take note of every experience so that when you reflect, you can reminisce on everything that you learned.

Regardless of whether the goal or vision is achieved, progress is always made. Don't get down on yourself, because progress is progression.

Day 14 "Always focus on the bigger picture; life is prettier that way."

As Queens, we have a tendency to look at the one wrinkle on our forehead, or the width of our nose versus our entire face. By centralizing one simple flaw, we magnify that, and then classify ourselves as something that we aren't.

Imperfection is everywhere, but that is what makes us unique. Just as our imperfections are unique, whether that be physically, mentally, or emotionally, we can't just focus on that one problem and make that the center of our being. Continue to look at the bigger picture, and change your view on life.

Day 15 "It is easier to love than it is to hate."

During my time after college, I faced several different challenges. While some were big and others not as important as some before, I found myself beginning to hate life and the hand that I was continuously dealt. However, after beginning to *hate* life, and *hate* what some of the consequences of my struggle brought, I wanted to seek a new mindset—one that required *love,* and one that didn't make me *feel* continued misery.

Although you may dislike what you're going through right now, it won't last forever. And it will be easier to get through once you learn to love what it is you're going through, because it is molding you into a better person in the end.

Day 16 "If it is meant to be, then it will be. No force. No struggle."

I am a firm believer of what you work for, you get; meaning that the goals you set, you will achieve. This is not to say that you won't be rerouted in the process of getting to the goal, but in the end, you will still get to the goal.

Queen, you must remember that your dreams are achievable as long as you don't force it. There is a thing called natural, raw talent, that most individuals have. It is something that comes natural and cannot be made up. You have to tap into that and use it. When I say that there should be no force or no struggle, I simply mean that what is for you is just for you! You won't have to manipulate or maneuver it. It is simply for you. Don't question it.

Day 17 "Be humble. Be selfless. Be different."

Queen, you will meet many people, but you must remember who you are. While you continue to keep your identity, always be humble, selfless, and different. You don't have to conform to what people are doing, how they are acting, or to what they are watching or listening to. You must only conform to you. Be you. Love you. Do you.

Day 18 "Your tolerance level is highlighted in every situation you face."

Have you ever witnessed a young toddler panting and crying in the grocery store line, due to not being able to get that piece of candy or small toy that they see? I can recall, several times, witnessing this as I went into different stores. However, the reaction from the mother or guardian is always a little different. Some parents cave in and get the item, and the child stops crying, while other parents refuse, and the child continues to cry.

This situation, like many others that you may witness, are a true reflection of your character. In this case, there is no right or wrong party, but you are welcome to cast your opinions based on what you believe you would do in that scenario. But still, there is no right or wrong, but based on what we see, one would pass judgement.

Queen, as you face different circumstances, remember that it isn't about the right or wrong, but about what people see. Refuse to argue over something openly in which people can cast judgement; instead, stand firm, and do what is best for you.

Day 19 "Life will throw you darts, but you must throw back shots."

Remember, you are strong. You are brilliant. You are unique. You will surpass your own expectations. As life throws you darts of pain, emotional ups and downs, family issues, and loss of friends, continue to combat that with remembering who you are. You are a lioness. You are a warrior. You are a gem. You are intelligent. You are *Queen*.

Day 20 "Rome wasn't built in a day; take your time and enjoy the process."

We live in a microwave society. This society has taught us that we need stuff right now, and it must be perfect. I hate to break it to you, but that is not how life works. That is not how your dreams will turn into reality. That is not how you will get everything that you were hoping and praying for. However, the way you get to everything that you've been hoping for is to build it, brick by brick; meaning that you are going to have to stack some things, lift some things, build up some things, and move things around for your building to fully form.

There are no instant buildings like our instant grits at the local grocery store. But if you take your time, that masterpiece will soon be the building of your dreams.

Day 21 "People will show you who they are, so stop giving them chances!"

Remember when I told you that your circle of friends was pivotal to your success? Well, this also goes along with new friends and new relationships that you begin to form as you find your way through life. As a queen, there is always a glowing light around you. With this light, you will attract some good people, and maybe even a few bad people. In order to see if those people are meant to be in your life or not, one must listen to what that person is saying. Don't get clouded by the title of their jobs, or by their social status, or even by the types of clothes and shoes they wear. Listen to their character, and let that shine a light on whether you want to continue to give them your energy.

As a Queen, you will encounter many people, but only a few are meant to be in your close circle of growing, thriving, uplifting people that you are around every day.

Day 22 "You may have to disappoint some people to get to your goals."

Disappointment is good. I repeat: Disappointment is good!!!

Oftentimes, when we hear the words, "I am disappointed in you," it comes from someone we care about. And this usually hurts us because we don't want to disappoint anyone that we care for or that cares for us. But the type of disappointment I am referring to is when our parents, close relatives, and friends have certain expectations for us, which we don't have for ourselves, and we disappoint them by not following their goals but by going toward our own. That disappointment is okay!

As a queen, you must realize that you have been gifted with a certain skills and a mindset that a lot of people will not understand, but that's okay. The main focus that you have to remember is that in some cases, your goals come first, and people's opinions come second.

Day 23 "Problems will never be solved, unless you hit the problem head on."

I'm the type of person that usually runs away at the slightest sign of confrontation. I typically want everything to be all roses and happy faces, but that is not how the world works. Some problems that you face may be uncomfortable, and they may be new, but you still have to treat them with the same attitude: I will get over this, and this will work out in my best interest.

But running from your problems and not addressing them doesn't solve anything.

Day 24 "Love the skin you're in young princess; soon, you will be a Queen."

Simply love where you're at now, and smile at where it is that you are soon to go.

When I was in the 11th grade, I couldn't wait to be a senior. Then, when I was a senior, I couldn't wait to go to college. Once I got into college, I couldn't wait to graduate and get a *real job*. After I got this real job, I couldn't wait to go back to school to strengthen my skills. But during each of these phases, I was always in a rush to do something. I was always so eager to get to the next thing that I never enjoyed the thing right in front of me.

Whatever phase you're in, just enjoy it; because you will soon be where you've dreamed of being all along.

Chapter 4

Academic Enrichment

*"I have learned over the years that
when one's mind is made up; this diminishes fear;
knowing what must be done does away with fear."*
– Rosa Parks

Introduction

Your academic development is very crucial at any age. I always admire how high school seniors prepare their photos upon graduating, ensuring that their hair, suit, dress, and shoes are exactly like they picture it. What's even more amazing is when these same individuals venture off to college and repeat that same scenario prior to their college graduation, with photo shoots, dinner reservations, and invitations in the mail.

While the final product of graduating is critical, we can't only talk about and celebrate that final moment; we must look at the steps it takes to get there. Graduation is great, but what about freshman, sophomore, and junior year? What about the teachers you endured? And what about the friends you made, and the study groups you attended or didn't attend? What about every term paper you wrote and revised ten times? We can't forget about everything that brought us to that great moment of hearing our name being blasted over an intercom as we walked gracefully across the stage.

While some of you may have just walked across the stage, there are others that are still preparing. As you are preparing for that new job or that next semester, I challenge you to reflect on the things you experienced. What would you have done differently, and how would that have made things better?

An educated Queen isn't the one that holds several degrees. An educated Queen is a Queen who understands the importance of trials and tests. She is the one that has endured and sustained. She is the one that has not given up. She is the one that knows the importance of a career versus just holding a job. She is the one that is taking her education by force, and not accepting anything less.

Have you given up? As you read through the next set of quotes, I encourage you to use them and apply them to your academic and career pursuits.

I'm rooting for you, Queen. It's never too late to learn something new.

Day 25 "Stay ready so you don't have to get ready!"

When you get a chance, post this quote wherever you can: *Stay ready so that you don't have to get ready.* This can be applied to any area of your life, such as your job, relationship, organization, or new business move. Simply put, this quote goes for everything. Sometimes we are unable to reach the opportunities that are placed in front of us, because we aren't prepared for them. The time we take waiting for an opportunity is also the time that we should be preparing for that specific opportunity or any other potential opportunity that could be coming our way.

Stay ready!!!!

Day 26 "Treat your first exam as if it is your FINAL exam."

When it comes to exams, mid-terms, qualifying exams, licensing exams, or whatever test that you will have to take, you must remember this quote. If we treat our first exam as if it were our last, we would be more prone to studying and not procrastinating. We would be more inclined to miss the social gathering, and get an extra night's rest for the test. Furthermore, we would be more open to attending a tutorial session, rather than not attending and simply studying on our own.

Queen, when you take the initiative to put your study habits first, you are ultimately setting yourself up for success in more areas than just academic enrichment—you are setting yourself up for success in life. Even if you've graduated and surpassed all of your standardized tests, think of how you're being tested at your job, in your family, and also in your relationships. Treat these tests with care and preparation.

You will win.

Day 27 "Trust in what you've studied; don't overthink it!"

Don't overthink what you have already prepared for, Queen. Oftentimes, we believe that we are ready, know that we are ready, and feel that we are ready. And still, when that moment or dream comes, we still question it. Know that what you have been preparing for is what you will get. Know that what you've been preparing for is on the way.

Day 28 "You can think yourself out of a tough situation."

Oftentimes, our thoughts can take us places that we aren't even supposed to go to. You have to remember that your mindset is under your control. No one else can tell you what to think or how to think. You have to do that on your own.

As your thoughts may sometimes get overwhelming, and it may seem as if you have no way out, remember to take a deep breath, pause for a second, and then begin again. The situation may appear to be big. That test may appear to be hard. That teacher may act as if she doesn't like you. But you must think your way through.

Day 29 "Start what you need to start, and remember to finish what you need to finish."

You can only begin at one place. Set your eyes first on where you need to start, and then on where you need to finish. Don't spread yourself so thin that you don't even want to begin. As you pursue coursework, start with 2 to 3 classes. With studying, start with two hours a day in the morning or evening. If you need to finish a paper, break it into pieces, from the intro to the conclusion, until you reach the final product.

Simply put, Queen, begin somewhere. Don't try to eat the whole elephant, but take it one piece at a time until you finish it.

Day 30 "Girl, keep it moving; keep it pushing."

You will find yourself in many situations that require your immediate attention, while others won't need your attention at all. With that being said, you must learn to move on from certain situations. Not everything or everyone deserves a response from you, nor are you obligated to give them one.

Day 31 "Good things come to those who WORK."

When I first started undergrad, I had a vision for myself. However, with that vision, I was missing a key ingredient. That ingredient was *work ethic*. Kind of like a cake with no eggs, it will not rise, nor will you want to eat it. With your visions, they will never come true unless you put in the effort to actually paint that picture.

In order to make your dreams a reality, you must put in the work. Again, I repeat: You must put in the work.

Day 32 "You must detach, detox, and deprogram to meet your educational goals."

Detach from your mistakes.

Detox all of the negative energy that may stem from taking the class, or from the assumptions that go along with it.

Deprogram your mind of anything that doesn't correlate with your vision of completing the goal.

Day 33 "Be flexible—not angry but flexible."

Oftentimes, when we are faced with a variety of situations that hit us all at once, we tend to get angry. During that anger, we tend to lash out. Furthermore, when we are lashing out, we say things that we probably don't mean, and we regret saying them.

Queen, you must be flexible. There will be times when you think to yourself, "Why am I the only one that is flexible?" And this question will loop in your mind a million times, but I'm here to tell you that you may never get that answer. Sometimes you have to be the bigger person, and in doing that, you cannot get angry and stay angry—you have to be flexible.

Day 34 "Every relationship has 3 components: the couple, the family, and the friends. Who will you listen to?"

Keep your relationships consistent. Keep your decisions consistent, and you will always be consistent. As you continue to grow in your journey, you will learn which of these three components matter most, in certain situations. Like we discussed in the previous chapter, you will disappoint people, but that doesn't always mean that you're the one in the wrong. Some people will only love you as long as you're doing *what they want*. That's not real love at all.

Queen, continue to remember these three components as you soar to new heights, and this will help you add to and multiply your continued happiness.

Day 35 "First you must make it. Then you must master it. Then you matter!"

Queen, you must set a goal. Then, you achieve that goal. Then, you will flourish in that goal. When you decide to conquer things based on what your goals and visions are for yourself, that is when you have truly mastered your purpose.

Remember, the things that you achieve along your academic journey are not solely for your own benefit, but they are to help a greater cause.

Day 36 "Know who you are so that you're not so easily defined."

Remember who you are. You are greatness. You are excellence. You are one in a million. You are worth far more than rubies and gold. You are intelligence. You are absolutely everything that exemplifies immaculate substance.

Queen, remember who you are. When people try to put labels on you, just remember who you are. You are a force be reckoned with. It's not about your occupation, your dress size, your last name, or even your zip code. It's about what you have inside, and what shines out. Don't let this world define you. Pick a title, and run with it.

Day 37 "Make this the year of learning, listening, and laughing."

You have to live like all of your dreams are already a reality.

You have to live like every door that you thought would close has now been opened.

You have to live like this is your moment right now.

You have to live like you're already walking in what you've worked so hard for.

Make this year, and every year from now on, a learning, listening, and laughing year. You may not see it yet, but you have to live in it. Smile, and keep on pushing. Learn, and keep on learning.

Chapter 5

Extraordinary Queen

"Embrace what makes you unique,
even if it makes others uncomfortable.
I didn't have to become perfect,
because I've learned throughout my journey
that perfection is the enemy of greatness."
— **Janelle Monae**

Introduction

Yay! You've made it to the final chapter. Living life like a Queen is tough. As you can see, I've faced several different situations that have caused me to question my goals, my visions, and my character, but I still continued to persist. That is exactly what we all have to do. We all must continue—continue and continue again. A real Queen isn't born overnight. A real Queen is developed through the crushing, life shattering, unbearable moments in which she wants to give up, but she doesn't. A Queen is developed in her happiest times and her worst times. A queen is developed when she is given a label that she refuses to adhere to. More importantly, a real queen is developed differently, and the way they are shaped is what makes them so unique, and that's why I am so happy to be able to talk to the Queen that is you.

Again, you are phenomenal, stunning, intelligent, brilliant, hardworking, and everything above amazing. You are ultimately extraordinary. Continue to rock your crown and to live on purpose, and to live like the true Queen that you have been this entire time.

Day 38 "Let me adjust my crown and get my day started."

Hey, Queen; by now, I hope that you've been able to see how we relate. I think that at some point, we all realize that we are not alone in this journey; that there are other women that have faced some of the same trials, setbacks, and triumphs as we have—just from a different perspective.

With this quote in mind, I want you to stop what you're doing, and look at yourself in the mirror. If you don't have a mirror, pull out your iPhone, Android, or smart tablet, and open up the photo app. Once that's done, I want you to snap a quick selfie of yourself, and get it printed. Post this picture somewhere you can look at it daily, so that you can look back and say that it was the day you decided to wear and keep your crown tilted high and not low. You will remember this day as the day you decided to always keep your crown on, because you recognized who you are and what you are worth.

Queen, you must always wear your crown.

Day 39 "Your worth is not found in your education, career, relationships, jean size, or bank account. Your true worth lies within."

Know your worth. Society has done a good job on us by making us believe that our value is in our money, clothing brands, and what seat we sit in at the office. None of those things hold any real value, but once you truly discover your value within, that's when you understand who you are and what you bring to the table.

Day 40 "The three most powerful R's in a relationship: Reload, Renew, and Resolute."

The relationships that you develop with others are important, but so is the relationship that you develop with yourself. Reload. Sometimes we take on too much, and we get upset with ourselves for not completing things as well as we would have if we didn't take on so much. We must reload ourselves with positive energy, positive vibes, positive thoughts, and positive people. Renew. We have to renew our minds. Yes, we know who we are and what we are capable of, but at times, we all need a refresher. Renew your mind and your thinking so that you can press forward consistently, so that you can get all the things that you want. The final thing is resolute. According to Webster's dictionary, this is defined as admirably purposeful, determined, and unwavering; meaning that you have to be unmoved by what life hands you, and stay caught up in the race that you are in with yourself, to be the best that you can possibly be.

The best relationship is the one that you develop with yourself first, so that you can have phenomenal relationships with other people.

Day 41 "Always remember the C-word, which is communicate."

You must always communicate. Oftentimes, we get so caught up in a "getting over things," and "I'm not worried about it," mindset that we never communicate our thoughts. The best way to get everything out is to let it out. This can be by writing in a journal, or talking with a close friend, or even with a mentor. But you must communicate your thoughts, or they will forever be thoughts, good or bad, which could lead to unanswered healing.

Day 42 "Don't be fooled; you got this—just be patient."

I usually spend 5–6 days a week at the gym. When I first started going, I hated it. I wanted to hurry up and get done so that I could check it off my list for the day. However, as I continued to go to the gym, I noticed that I became accustomed to wanting to speed things up and not actually do the workout to its fullest extent. With that, I was not experiencing the fullest results either. Once I slowed down and did not rush through my workout, I began to see the results that I desired.

Queen, you have to be patient and consistent. You have what it takes, but you must be patient and enjoy the process.

Day 43 "Enjoy this journey you're on...it's the only one that you will get."

You only get one life. I repeat: You only get one life. With that, you only get one journey. That journey may have different paths, with different people at each turn, and may even have some construction zones that you may not be able to venture toward, but it is still your journey, and you must live it for *you*.

Day 44 "You win 365, only if you want to win 365."

Every day is important. There are no such things as good days and bad days; just days in which opportunities open and close. Utilize your 365 in a way that is most beneficial for you, so that your good days and bad days turn into more opportunities, and continued opportunities.

Day 45 "Your biggest competition: yourself. Your biggest downfall: yourself."

When we look at ourselves, we see two images. The first is the one staring back at us, and the other is the one that our mind tells us we are. I believe that these two images can be hard to deal with at times because we get so caught up in who we want, need, or wish to be, and we forget about the person standing right in front of us. I believe that you have to enjoy the process. Embrace who you are now. Love who you are now. Smile at who you are now, so that you will really enjoy who you want to be.

As you continue to stare at who you are and who you will soon be, remember that you are your biggest competition. The goal is to be better than who you were yesterday, so that you can get to who you are trying to become. No competing and comparing to others—simply be you.

Day 46 "When you find your why, you find your way."

When I was young, I knew that I wanted to help people. I knew that I wanted to impact someone's life, and I wanted to make a difference in the world. I also knew that this would not be easy and that I would face a few bumps along the road. As you come into the person of your purpose, there will be many things that seem like roadblocks, but they are really leading you on your path to where you're supposed to be.

When you find the why in your purpose, it will lead you to your way. Every setback, mishap, and minor delay does not mean that you aren't doing exactly what you're supposed to be doing, when you're supposed to be doing it. Stay consistent, Queen, and make room for this path ahead.

Day 47 "Every season is for a reason. Be grateful. Be mindful."

I've learned not to question everything. Sounds hard, right? Well, for me, it was one of the hardest things that I've ever had to do. I wanted to know *why this* and *why that*. I wanted exact answers for everything. As I continued to grow and learn, I realized that sometimes you won't get those answers that you're longing for in order to feel complete. Sometimes the greatest answers are those found in not knowing. Now, don't get me wrong; I still seek the reason for certain things, but I've learned to not let it weigh in on me as it would have once before.

Queen, be delighted in whatever season you're in—whether it be a broken season, a cleansing season, or an unanswered season. Just know that there is a reason for it, and whatever your response is, will determine how long that season will last.

Day 48 "We are different, not because of our location, but because of our destination."

As I mentioned before, we are all Queens, but we are at different points within our lives. I encourage you to find fellow Queens that you can work with, grow with, and build with. This will make the journey that much easier, and you will find strength throughout the process to help someone else as well.

Day 49 "Life is too short to be anything but happy, so get to your *happy*."

Get to your *happy*. Whatever that is, I want you to discover it. I am still learning what makes me happy and what works best for me. Throughout every book that I've read, or article that I've researched, scientists still conclude that happiness starts with you. Yes, material things can cause happiness, for a moment. But moments do not last forever. The happiness brewing in you is enough to sustain a lifetime. Tap into that, so that you can truly live life like you're supposed to.

Day 50 "Strive to always move forward; you won't achieve anything looking back."

Queen, you must always move forward, regardless of the setback or the setup. Keep moving forward. It is easier said than done, but if you quit now, you will never see how great you can be. I'm rooting for you, and all the other Queens out there are rooting for you as well. Keep your eyes forward.

Conclusion

Thank you for choosing this book. I am always reading, learning, and talking with Queens on how we can become better as a unit. This book is just a glimpse of what I've experienced, and quotes that have helped me along the way. I hope that you are able to use this book in some way to encourage other Queens, and to continue living your best life right now as a Queen. Remember, I am rooting for you!

www.ingramcontent.com/pod-product-compliance
Lightning Source LLC
Chambersburg PA
CBHW061047050726
47592CB00004B/1616